FRANCIS FRITH'S
TOWN & CITY
MEMORIES

BLACKBURN

ALAN DUCKWORTH was born in Queensbury in Yorkshire and worked for some time in the textile and iron founding industries. He was a student at Leeds Polytechnic and moved to Lancashire in 1971. He has worked in a number of libraries, including Darwen, Chorley, Accrington and Lancaster. He is currently Assistant Librarian in the Community History Department of Blackburn Library.
He has had a number of books published including the acclaimed Lancashire cycling guide, 'The Man with No Bike Clips'.

CORPORATION PARK 1895 35729

FRANCIS FRITH'S
TOWN & CITY
MEMORIES

BLACKBURN

ALAN DUCKWORTH

FRANCIS FRITH'S
TOWN & CITY
MEMORIES

First published as Blackburn, A Photographic History of your Town
in 2002 by Black Horse Books, an imprint of The Francis Frith Collection
Revised edition published in the United Kingdom in 2005 by
The Francis Frith Collection as Blackburn, Town and City Memories
Limited Hardback Edition ISBN 1-84589-051-5
Paperback Edition ISBN 1-85937-986-9

British Library Cataloguing in Publication Data

Blackburn
Town and City Memories
Alan Duckworth

The Francis Frith Collection®
Frith's Barn, Teffont,
Salisbury, Wiltshire SP3 5QP
Tel: +44 (0) 1722 716 376
Email: info@francisfrith.co.uk
www.francisfrith.co.uk

Aerial photographs reproduced under licence from Simmons Aerofilms Limited
Historical Ordnance Survey maps reproduced under licence from Homecheck.co.uk

Printed and bound in England

Front Cover: **BLACKBURN, SUDELL CROSS 1895** 35726t
The colour-tinting in this image is for illustrative purposes only,
and is not intended to be historically accurate

Every attempt has been made to contact copyright holders of illustrative material.
We will be happy to give full acknowledgement in future editions for any items not
credited. Any information should be directed to The Francis Frith Collection.

AS WITH ANY HISTORICAL DATABASE, THE FRANCIS FRITH ARCHIVE IS CONSTANTLY BEING
CORRECTED AND IMPROVED, AND THE PUBLISHERS WOULD WELCOME INFORMATION ON
OMISSIONS OR INACCURACIES

FRANCIS FRITH'S
TOWN & CITY
MEMORIES

CONTENTS

F rancis Frith, Victorian founder of the world-famous photographic archive, was a devout Quaker and a highly successful Victorian businessman. By 1860 he was already a multi-millionaire, having established and sold a wholesale grocery business in Liverpool. He had also made a series of pioneering photographic journeys to the Nile region. The images he returned with were the talk of London. An eminent modern historian has likened their impact on the population of the time to that on our own generation of the first photographs taken on the surface of the moon.

Frith had a passion for landscape, and was as equally inspired by the countryside of Britain as he was by the desert regions of the Nile. He resolved to set out on a new career and to use his skills with a camera. He established a business in Reigate as a specialist publisher of topographical photographs.

Frith lived in an era of immense and sometimes violent change. For the poor in the early part of Victoria's reign work was a drudge and the hours long, and ordinary people had precious little free time. Most had not travelled far beyond the boundaries of their own town or village. Mass tourism was in its infancy during the 1860s, but during the next decade the railway network and the establishment of Bank Holidays and half-Saturdays gradually made it possible for the working man and his family to enjoy holidays and to see a little more of the world. With characteristic business acumen, Francis Frith foresaw that these new tourists would enjoy having souvenirs to commemorate their days out. He began selling photo-souvenirs of seaside resorts and beauty spots, which the Victorian public pasted into treasured family albums.

Frith's aim was to photograph every town and village in Britain. For the next thirty years he travelled the country by train and by pony and trap, producing fine photographs of seaside resorts and beauty spots that were keenly bought by millions of Victorians.

THE RISE OF FRITH & CO

Each photograph was taken with tourism in mind, the small team of Frith photographers concentrating on busy shopping streets, beaches, seafronts, picturesque lanes and villages. They also photographed buildings: the Victorian and Edwardian eras were times of huge building activity, and town halls, libraries, post offices, schools and technical colleges were springing up all over the country. They were invariably celebrated by a proud Victorian public, and photo souvenirs – visual records – published by F Frith & Co were sold in their hundreds of thousands. In addition, many new commercial buildings such as hotels, inns and pubs were photographed, often because their owners specifically commissioned Frith postcards or prints of them for re-sale or for publicity purposes.

In order to gain some understanding of the scale of Frith's business one only has to look at the catalogue issued by Frith & Co in 1886: it runs to some 670 pages. By 1890 Frith had created the greatest specialist photographic publishing company in the world, with over 2,000 stockists! The picture on the right shows the Frith & Co display board on the wall of the stockist at Ingleton in the Yorkshire Dales (left of window). Beautifully constructed with a mahogany frame and gilt inserts, it displayed a dozen scenes.

POSTCARD BONANZA

The ever-popular holiday postcard we know today took many years to appear, and F Frith & Co was in the vanguard of its development. Postcards became a hugely popular means of communication and sold in their millions. Frith's company took full advantage of this boom and soon became the major publisher of photographic view postcards.

Francis Frith died in 1898 at his villa in Cannes, his great project still growing. His sons Eustace and Cyril continued their father's monumental task, expanding the number of views offered to the public and recording more and more places in Britain, as the coasts and countryside were opened up to mass travel. The archive Frith created continued in business for another seventy years. By 1970 it contained over a third of a million pictures of 7,000 cities, towns and villages. The massive photographic record Frith has left to us stands as a living monument to a special and very remarkable man.

This book shows Blackburn as it was photographed by this world-famous archive at various periods in its development over the past 150 years. Every photograph was taken for a specific commercial purpose, which explains why the selection may not show every aspect of the town landscape. However, the photographs, compiled from one of the world's most celebrated archives, provide an important and absorbing record of your town.

INTRODUCTION

Celia Fiennes toured England at the end of the 17th century. She did not visit Blackburn. Thirty years later Daniel Defoe toured the country. He visited Bolton, Bury and Preston, and viewed Pendle from afar, but he did not come to Blackburn either. At this time Blackburn was the market town for north-east Lancashire, and had a population of a little over 5,000.

In 1933 J B Priestley made his 'English Journey', and he did visit Blackburn. In the 200 years since Defoe's time, remarkable things had happened to the town. Handloom weaving as an adjunct to small-scale farming had been practised in the area for centuries, and quite extensively since the 18th century. With the invention of the power loom, the warehouses, which had been used to store the cloth pieces brought in by the handloom weavers, were converted into mills. Power looms were installed, and the formerly independent handloom weavers became employees. Their remote cottages had to be given up, and new homes, long rows of terraced houses, were built near the mills.

There was plenty of coal to be had fairly locally, and the damp climate suited the spinning and weaving of cotton fibres; and so the cotton industry boomed in Blackburn. The population had soared to a peak of 133,000 by 1911. At the time of Priestley's visit, however, the industry was in decline. It was a world-wide slump, but Blackburn, having relied heavily on just one industry, was hit particularly badly. Priestley described Blackburn as 'a sad-looking town', but added:

'The streets are not filled with men dismally loafing about. You do not see abandoned shops, which look as if they are closed for ever, down every street. Everything that was there before the slump, except the businesses themselves, is struggling on. In nearly every instance, the whole town is there, just as it was, but not in the condition it was. Its life is suffering from a deep internal injury'.

Blackburn stands on the river of the same name. It may be that the name means simply 'black stream', although in the Domesday Book it is written 'Blacheborne' and may be a reference to bleaching. If poor communications was the reason for its lack of visits by itinerant chroniclers of the English scene, then the industrialisation of Blackburn soon remedied

THE INDUSTRIAL AREA c1955 B111004

Taken from the viewing platform on the recently demolished water tank at Revidge, this is a view of Blackburn before the cotton industry went into a terminal decline. How many chimneys are there in this shot? The one in the centre was the tallest one in town, and was the one at the refuse destructor.

BROWNHILL c1960 B111028

The northern expansion of Blackburn along Whalley New Road led ultimately to the creation of new housing estates in areas like Brownhill. This is a view down Brownhill Drive looking towards the Brownhill Arms. The chimney on the left is at Ramsgreave Laundry in Pleckgate Road, owned by the Haydock Brothers.

the situation. The Leeds to Liverpool Canal reached Blackburn from the east in 1810 and from the west in 1816. The Turnpike Trust built Whalley New Road in 1820 and Preston New Road in 1825. The railway to Preston opened in 1846, to Accrington in 1848, to Burnley and Colne in 1850, and to Chorley and Wigan in 1869.

And along these lines of communication came those vital raw materials, coal and cotton, and perhaps the most significant raw

INTRODUCTION

By 1836, in his 'History of the County Palatine of Lancaster', Edward Baines was able to describe the town thus:

'In the early stages of the cotton business, the inhabitants in general were indigent and scantily provided; (and this is still the case, so far as the hand-loom weavers are concerned;) but decisive proofs of wealth now appear in this place on every hand: handsome new erections are continually rising up, public institutions for the improvement of the mind and the extension of human happiness are rapidly increasing; and this place, at one time proverbial for its rudeness and want of civilisation, may now fairly rank, in point of opulence and intelligence, with many of the principal towns in the kingdom'.

The slump observed by J B Priestley was a temporary, if significant, setback. It was recognised that the former laissez-faire approach to the cotton industry could not be maintained, and that a more organised approach was needed. An Act of Parliament to control the industry was proposed, but the Second World War intervened, and the demand for military clothing and equipment revived the industry.

After the war demand for cotton goods remained strong; the main problem was shortage of labour. Many employees had left to do war-work, and did not return. The solution was found by recruiting people from India, Pakistan and from among the displaced Asian population of East Africa.

The fortunes of the cotton industry in Blackburn can be gauged by the number of looms in operation. The high point was reached in 1917, with 94,000 looms. By 1937 there were 35,000. After the war there was a slight increase, but from 1956 onwards there was a steady decline; by 1976 there were only 2,100. To all intents and purposes, the cotton industry and the 20th century came to an end together. By 1999 there were just 100 looms running in the town.

Again, communications have come to the town's rescue. The construction of the M65 in the mid 1990s linked Blackburn to the motorway network, bringing Manchester Airport to within a 40-minute drive and Liverpool Docks to within 90 minutes. Paper, chemicals, rubber and plastic industries are now all represented in the borough, and the town presents as busy and as prosperous a face as ever it did in its prime as a cotton town.

material of all: human labour. The proliferation of mills sucked people in like a fire sucks in oxygen. They came from the rural areas nearby, from rural areas further afield, from Scotland and from Ireland. It was their labour which made Blackburn prosperous.

LAMMACK c1950 B111005

Another shot taken from the 'tank' at Revidge, this time looking north away from the town. Blackburn is expanding, houses have appeared along Lammack Road and along Whinney Lane, branching off it to the right. On the far left is Blackburn golf course.

KING WILLIAM STREET

The reign of King William IV (the original 'Silly Billy') from 1830 to 1837 was brief compared to that of his niece and successor Queen Victoria; however, he was a popular monarch. Thus, when Blackburn began town centre improvements in 1832, his name was adopted for the new street constructed from Sudell Cross at the bottom of Preston New Road to the Market Cross in Church Street. Old shops and warehouses that were already centuries old were demolished as new shops were built along what had previously been known as Livesey Street, which was now absorbed by the new thoroughfare.

Thus began a shift of focus away from Church Street, which had been the commercial heart of the town. This trend was confirmed when the new market house was erected in 1848 (34307 opposite). It was built in King William Street on a site formerly known as Sudell's Croft, and measured 180 feet by 90 feet. The architect was Terence Flanagan, and the contractor was the local builder Robert Ibbotson. William Yates's foundry supplied the iron for the framework and the roof supports. A clock tower was also built. It was 18 feet square and 72 feet high, with a ball at the top. At noon every day the ball rose up its pole until at one o'clock it reached the top; then it descended quickly, and a cannon was fired warning the workers, most of whom would not have had a watch, to return to work.

Robert Whittle, in his book 'Blackburn as it Is' published in 1852, gives his own impression of the building:

'The style of the architecture is that of the early Italian palazzo; a style that is truly magnificent, and at the same time elegant in itself. It is due west as to the front and due east as to the rear. In fact, the style is chaste, and completely unique in appearance. Its internal appearance is imposing

THE MARKET AND THE TOWN HALL 1894 34307

This is King William Street, with the Market Hall clock on the right. The buildings on the left, the site of Marks and Spencer today, were known as the Peel Buildings in honour of Sir Robert Peel. Note the lack of wheeled traffic in King William Street, making the scene reminiscent of today. This was later to change as vehicles proliferated and caused congestion, leading to eventual pedestrianisation.

King William Street

The Market c1965 B111053

A quantum leap from the old market. This shows the Salford/Penny Street end of the market with its 'space age' styling. It may look dated now, but in the 1960s this was up-to-the-minute design, along with the high-rise flats at Larkhill in the background and the modernisation of Thwaites Brewery going on at the extreme right. Note the size and prominence of the Ying Kin Chinese restaurant. At the time the English were just acquiring a taste for foreign food, and 'going for a Chinese' was the thing to do. Later, Indian restaurants would supersede the Chinese ones.

This rear view of the Market Hall shows the three roof spans. Note that the ball on the tower is near the top of its pole as one o'clock approaches. The Borough Arms stands on the right.

from its great length, width, and height, but aerial and elegant in the extreme.'

The canvas-covered stalls in the market place (34307, pages 14-15, 34306, above) provided little protection for shoppers in Blackburn's frequent wet weather. A cascade of cold water down the back of your neck was all part of the shopping experience. It was this, along with the time-consuming task of erecting and dismantling stalls and clearing away rubbish, that led to the eventual building of the new shopping centre and market.

During 1870-72 a second market house intended for a fish market was built. In 1935 the interior of the market hall was remodelled, and the east end was completely rebuilt.

Before work could begin on the present market in the 1960s (B111053, opposite) the course of the River Blakewater had to be diverted. Plans for a new market and shopping centre were announced in May 1961, and the new market was begun on 1 November 1962. The old market hall was demolished, and with it on 30 December 1964 the much-loved market hall tower.

The town hall (43471, page 22, B111003, pages 20-21) became

THE MARKET c1965 B111062

Inside the new five-day market, with some well-known names of stall holders in view: A Holliday and Sons, who sold materials and buttons; Joe Littler, the butcher; and Joseph Haworth, who sold sweets and tobacco. Note the Granville Café on the balcony. This was run by J Cardwell and E Barnes.

KING WILLIAM STREET

the next jewel in King William Street's crown. It was erected during the years 1852-56. The architect was James Paterson, and the contractors were Richard Hacking and William Stones. Lord of the Manor Joseph Feilden laid the corner stone. It contained a police station, 18 cells, a large assembly room and a council chamber.

In 1851 there had been a proposal to build a cotton exchange on the site of the market cross. This scheme failed to materialise, and when the new town hall was completed, exchange business was held there on Wednesdays. The Manchester architect Mr Brakespear was engaged in 1860 to design a new exchange, and in 1865 the building opened (43478, page 23, and B111042, page 23). The building subsequently became a lecture hall, where Charles Dickens read from his work. Later still it was a cinema, being known successively as the Exchange Hall, the Majestic (B111042, page 23), the Essoldo and the Classic.

We may think of traffic noise as being a modern nuisance; but an item in the Blackburn Times in October 1908 tells us that traffic was a nuisance nearly 100 years ago, for it welcomes the installation of wood blocks in King William Street. Previously this had been the noisiest part of the town centre. The article expresses the hope that the new paving be extended as far as Sudell Cross, so as to reduce the traffic noise for concert-goers at the Exchange Hall.

Traffic congestion in King William Street had long been a problem, and in 1972 it was announced that the street would be closed. South-bound traffic from Preston New Road would be routed down Montague Street, and north-bound traffic would continue along Northgate. King William Street retains its pre-eminence as the focal point of the town centre, though the recent pedestrianisation of Church Street may shift the balance.

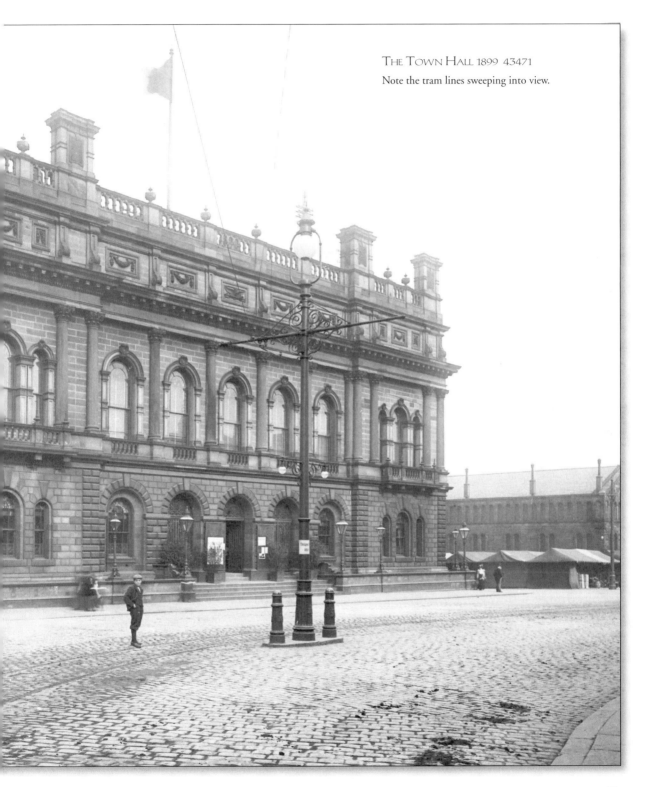

The Town Hall 1899 43471

Note the tram lines sweeping into view.

KING WILLIAM STREET

THE TOWN HALL c1955 B111003

This is how local historian W A Abram described the Town Hall: 'The west front, 120 feet wide, with an elevation of 63 feet, presents the main entrance in the centre, by three massive arched doorways. The front is emboldened by Corinthian columns resting upon a rusticated basement upholding a broad tablature surmounted by a perforated parapet' - an impressive piece of architecture. A half century after 43471 was taken (page 20-21), this photograph shows the blackened walls of the Town Hall, which demonstrate the effects of the thousands of smoking chimneys in the town, both industrial and domestic. Its original colour was restored when it was sandblasted in 1968.

Below: THE TOWN HALL c1955 B111042

Note the change of illumination outside the Town Hall. On the right is the Exchange Building in its incarnation as the Majestic Cinema. Davy Crockett is showing, and you could have had a seat in the stalls for one shilling (5p), or in the circle for one shilling and sixpence (7½p).

Bottom: THE EXCHANGE 1899 43478

The Exchange looks here much as it did when Charles Dickens ascended its steps to give his reading. The premises on the right advertising Whittle Springs Ales was W H Gregson's brewers' agents, later to become an office for Grant's whisky, the only one they had outside Scotland - a tribute to Blackburn's fondness for strong liquor. On the left was the Exchange Hotel.

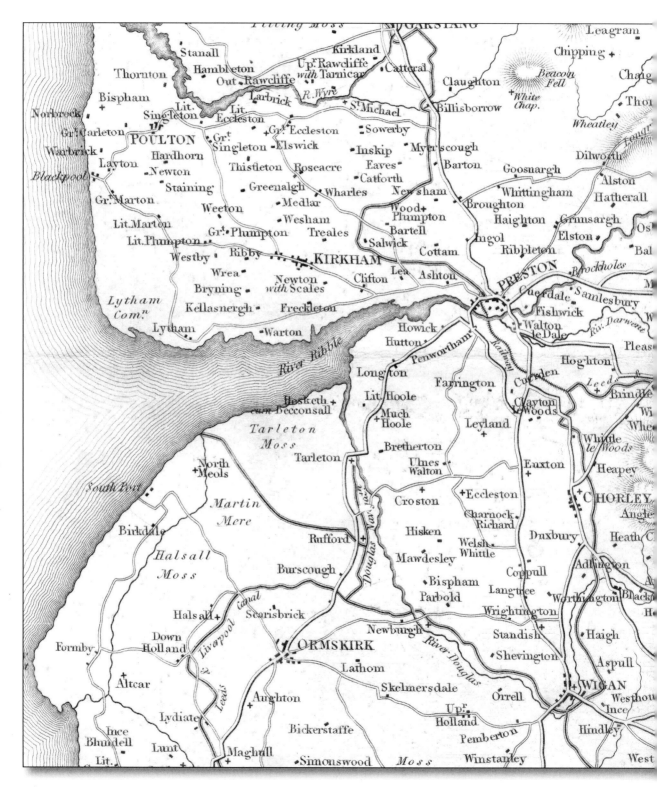

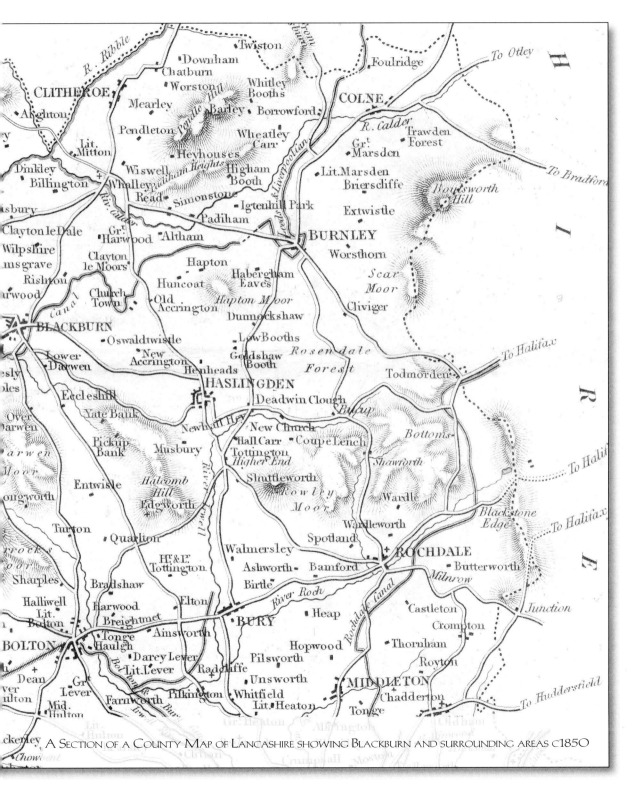

A Section of a County Map of Lancashire showing Blackburn and surrounding areas c1850

SUDELL CROSS TO SALFORD: A PERAMBULATION

Sudell Cross commemorates the Sudell family, who have been associated with Blackburn since the 16th century, when John Sudell held land at Oozebooth. It was Henry Sudell, born in 1864, who became the most successful and notable member of the family. A successful manufacturer and merchant, he was reputedly a millionaire. He built Woodfold Hall.

The 'Big Lamp' on the left of 35726 (right) was a gift to the town from Mayor Jack Smith in 1867. It was a favourite meeting place for couples, who would continue their tryst in Corporation Park. The 'Big Lamp' was considered a traffic hazard, and was later removed. The modern standard with its four lights in the middle of the roundabout (B111043, pages 30-31) only faintly echoes the glories of the 'Big Lamp'.

Sudell Cross was created when Preston New Road (34315, pages 32-33, 43477, pages 34-35, B111031, page 37) was built; before that it was merely the continuation of Northgate into Shear Brow. The bad state of the roads had been an impediment to the development of industry, and plans for a new road to Preston had been put forward in 1822. Henry Sudell promised to give the land required for the road, which passed through his estate. A Bill was introduced, and the Blackburn and Preston Turnpike Road and Bridge Act was passed in 1824. The project was beset by financial difficulties, but the new road opened in 1828.

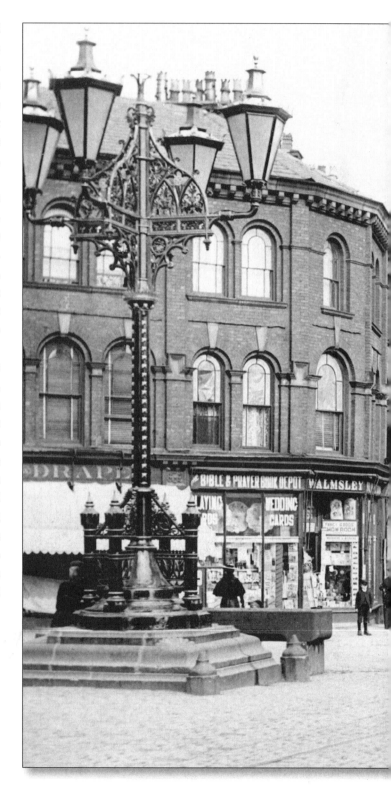

SUDELL CROSS TO SALFORD: A PERAMBULATION

SUDELL CROSS 1895 35726

A horse-drawn tram is rolling away down King William Street.
Notice the horse trough below the lamp standard - a journalist on
a local scandal sheet was once ducked in it by an irate reader.

SUDELL CROSS TO SALFORD: A PERAMBULATION

SUDELL CROSS c1901 43473

Note the overhead wires: the electric tram has arrived. Straw boaters and shirt sleeves give a warm weather feel to the photograph. The Grapes Hotel on the right had been quenching thirsts since Preston New Road opened eighty years earlier; sited at the top of Northgate, it was one of that street's sixteen inns.

SUDELL CROSS TO SALFORD: A PERAMBULATION

Church Street (B111038, page 36-37, and B111044, page 37) is the oldest street in the town. From Blackburn's earliest existence as a village or hamlet, there would have been dwellings on the banks of the Blakewater facing the church. It is a street that runs right through Blackburn's history, a street of memories and ghosts. The Market Cross stood here once at the junction with Darwen Street. John Paslew, Abbot of Whalley, who was executed in 1537 for his part in the Pilgrimage of Grace, had a town house here; the entrance to the much-missed Thwaites Arcade was in Church Street on the site of Abbot Paslew's house. A member of the ubiquitous Sudell family had a house here opposite the church gate early in the 18th century. Henry Feilden built a house here, which stood until 1882 - it was the Feildens' residence while in town. The recent pedestrianisation of Church Street and the installation of cotton-plant inspired sculptures restores to this ancient thoroughfare some of the tranquillity of earlier times, and may encourage quiet reflection.

The original Salford Bridge over the Blakewater was a narrow affair, barely 15 feet wide. In 1846, when the railway came to Blackburn, the river was covered over, and the bridge was extended to form part of Railway Road. It is said that Salford means safe ford, and there were once stepping stones in the river here to assist people to cross. But although the Blakewater presents a peaceful aspect today, in the past it could become an impassable torrent in bad weather. There have been a number of floods. Twelve people were drowned in 1792 when the river overflowed its banks, four people drowned in floods in 1792 and there was significant flooding in 1821, 1847 and 1901.

In 1882 Salford was again improved when a new railway station was erected. The original Salford Bridge had been something of a bottle-neck. An open space approached by broad thoroughfares was created, with handsomely-proportioned buildings like the new Bay Horse and the White Bull (B111046, page 40 and 43476, pages 38-39). The Bay Horse Inn (B111038, page 36-37) was built when Salford was improved in 1846, it was demolished in 1963. There had been an earlier inn of the same name there, a famous coaching inn, from where the coach to Manchester left every Monday, Wednesday and Friday. The new Theatre Royal opened in 1886 - it stood at the corner of Ainsworth Street.

In the 1840s Station Road, leading to the railway station, and

SUDELL CROSS c1955 B111043

The trams are gone, and the bus rules the highways. Among the premises to the left are Balmforth's the chemist's and Southworth's pet shop.

Bridge Street, which ran alongside the River Blakewater, took up the site now occupied by the Boulevard (B111037, pages 40-41). Between Station Road and Bridge Street was a timber yard owned by Thomas Duckworth. Overlooking the site was Spring

Hill Mill, which was built in 1797 by Anderton Bros. Jubilee Brewery occupied the area between Dandy Walk and Jubilee Street - this later became Jubilee Mill, popularly known as the Dandy Factory. It was attacked in 1826 by rioters, who blamed the factory system for their hardships: 212 power looms were smashed. Later still, the Railway Company bought the timber yard and created a spacious approach to the station. Blackburn Gas Works were built in Jubilee Street in 1819.

PRESTON NEW ROAD 1894 34315

This is the era of horse-drawn transport - the evidence is piled up at the side of the road. There are tram lines, but even these were horse-drawn at this time. The spire on the left belongs to St George's Presbyterian church, which opened in 1868 and was demolished in 1974.

SUDELL CROSS TO SALFORD: A PERAMBULATION

PRESTON, NEW ROAD 1899 43477

The electric tram standard dominates this scene, but horse-drawn traffic is still very much in evidence. Note the fine carriage on the right: perhaps the owner has been shopping at Aspinall's the chemist's, or choosing books at the West End Library, before being driven back to his or her villa residence further up Preston New Road.

SUDELL CROSS TO SALFORD: A PERAMBULATION

Blackburn's old Palace Theatre (B111037, page 40) opened in 1899; here Charlie Chaplin, Harry Lauder, George Formby and Gracie Fields appeared. The 'Great Houdini' appeared here too, and challenged the audience to bind him. William Hope Hodgson, a gymnasium owner and writer of eerie tales, accepted the challenge; he bound Houdini so securely that it was the early hours of the morning before he escaped, and even then, according to Hodgson, it was only with the help of a knife smuggled to him by his assistant. The Palace became a cinema in 1936 and was demolished in 1988.

The first railway line in Blackburn linked the town to Preston. It was built by the Blackburn and Preston Railway Company, later the East Lancashire Railway Company. The first sod was cut on 19 August 1844, and the line was officially opened on Whit Monday, 1 June 1846. The station was built on an area of waste land known as Stoney Butts. An extension to Accrington was opened on June 19 1848.

In 1844 the Blackburn, Darwen and Bolton Railway Company was formed to link the town with Bolton; this line was subsequently extended to Whalley, Clitheroe and Chatburn. A line to Chorley and Wigan was built by the Lancashire Union Railway in conjunction with the Lancashire and Yorkshire Railway, which opened in 1864.

The Boulevard took on the role of a transport interchange with the arrival of the tram. It was in 1881 that the Blackburn and Over

SUDELL CROSS TO SALFORD: A PERAMBULATION

Left:
CHURCH STREET c1955 B111038

A busy teatime scene with office workers making their way to the Boulevard for the bus home. On the left is Hilton's, the boot dealer's. On the right past Williams Deacon's bank is Henry Dodgson's, the costumier's.

Below Left:
PRESTON NEW ROAD c1955 B111031

A quiet view taken near the top of Preston New Road. On the right is the wall of Westholme School, and on the left are Billinge View and St Silas's vicarage. The trees are in full leaf - this is summer fifty years ago in one of the most attractive approaches to the town.

Below Right:
CHURCH STREET c1955 B111044

The Woolworth's on the left was one of the biggest branches in the north-west. The premises are now occupied by T J Hughes. Beyond Woolworth's were Adamson's the stationer's and the Golden Lion Hotel. The public toilets in the foreground were recently rediscovered when Church Street was being pedestrianised. Among the shops on the left are Saxone's shoe shop and Boots the chemist's.

SUDELL CROSS TO SALFORD: A PERAMBULATION

SALFORD BRIDGE 1899 43476

A view from Salford looking up Church Street. The building on the
far right is the Bay Horse; beyond is the office of Appleby and Sons,
millers, and beyond that the Royal Commercial Hotel, Astley's
the stationer's, Cowburn's the umbrella manufacturers and Beaty
Brothers the clothier's in the distance. On the left is the White Bull
Hotel - Miss E Cronkshaw was the landlady there at the time.

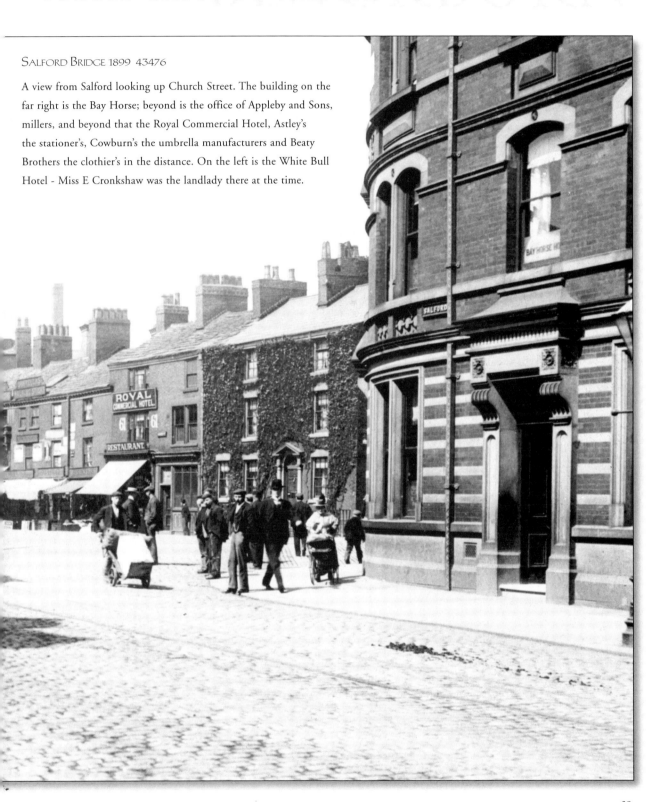

SUDELL CROSS TO SALFORD: A PERAMBULATION

Right: THE WHITE BULL HOTEL c1955 B111046

Salford roundabout is just in the foreground with the White Bull, and beyond is Baines and Allen, outfitters.

Below: THE BOULEVARD c1955 B111037

A scene from the golden age of bus transport, when there were conductors on the buses and queues that doubled back on themselves – and when you became expert at estimating how many could fit on a bus and know whether you'd have to wait for the next.

Darwen Tramways Company began operating their line from the Angel Inn in Darwen to St Peter Street in Blackburn. It was a steam tram, and in the following years steam trams began operating to Church (1887) and Blackburn cemetery (1888). Horse-drawn routes were set up to Preston New Road in 1888 and Witton Stocks in 1889. In 1898 Blackburn Corporation took over the tramway undertaking, and in 1899 the electrification of the system began. Tram services continued until 1949. They enjoyed a revival during the Second World War when petrol was difficult to obtain. The last tram, No 74, left the town for the depot at Intack on 3 September 1949.

Blackburn Corporation bought a fleet of 12 petrol-engined buses in 1929; they ran on the Arterial Road, Little Harwood,

London Road, Wensley Fold, Whitebirk and Accrington routes. A service to Darwen in conjunction with Darwen Corporation began in 1930. In 1935 the Corporation bought its first diesel-engined buses, and buses took over from trams on the Queens Park route. After the war, buses steadily replaced trams: on the Preston New Road route in 1946, the Wilpshire route in 1947 and the Church-Intack and Darwen routes in 1949.

If you ask anyone today where Darwen Street Bridge is, they will describe the railway bridge which crosses Darwen Street at the point where it joins Great Bolton Street. But Darwen Street Bridge is in fact nearer the town centre at the point where the road crosses the River Blakewater. Here was once the town's lock-up, which was known as the House of Correction. It was actually a cellar beneath

a shop, close to the river and infested with rats, and there was an adjoining cellar which was used as a gunpowder store. The unhappy prisoner thus had a choice of concerns: sudden flooding, or a stray spark finding its way next door.

Darwen Street (B111047, page 42) is second only to Church Street as an important and ancient thoroughfare, and it was second only to Northgate as a street of inns. There was the Bird in Hand, the Ship, the Eagle and Child, the Hare and Hounds, the Three Crowns, the Queen's Head, the Anchor, the Wheatsheaf, the Duke of York, a second White Bull and one of the oldest inns in Blackburn, the Legs of Man, formerly the Paslew Arms, patronised by pilgrims since the 14th century.

When the market was held in Church Street, stalls spilled over into Darwen Street as far down as Jubilee Street. It has been a street of shops ever since. In 1900 some of them, the ones in a block near the top of Darwen Street, Nos 19 to 21 (they included Poldings corn shop, Fish's newsagents, a woollen shop and a chemist) were demolished to make way for the new post office (B111047, page 42), which opened in November 1907. The last shop in the row, Carlisle's or the Old Bedding Shop, survived until 1924, when it was pulled down for a post office extension. In 1977 further old shops were demolished, and later the County Hotel and the Legs of Man followed. This allowed the council to realise their plan to open up Cathedral Close. Further landscaping and the recent pedestrianisation of Church Street, which sweeps round to the top of Darwen Street, has transformed this ancient corner of Blackburn.

SUDELL CROSS TO SALFORD: A PERAMBULATION

SUDELL CROSS TO SALFORD: A PERAMBULATION

Left:
THE BOULEVARD c1955 B111001

A view looking towards Salford with St John's Church in the background. The Adelphi Hotel alone remains of the buildings on the far right, which include the offices of London Assurance and Pearl Assurance. Beyond Kemsley House on the corner, home of the Northern Daily Telegraph, which had been going since 1887, were Barker, Son & Heins Ltd, piano dealers.

Below Left:
DARWEN STREET c1955 B111047

This is a view looking towards the town centre. On the right is the post office; it closed in 1972, and moved to premises in Ainsworth Street in the new shopping centre. The old building remained, and is now a pub called the Postal Order – it thus replaces at least one of Darwen Street's lost inns.

Below Right:
THE BOULEVARD 1902 48571

A tranquil scene. The little old lady in the foreground can take her time crossing the Boulevard when there is only the odd horse and cart to worry about. The fountain and flower-bed on the left were removed when the Boulevard was remodelled in the 1950s.

BLACKBURN FROM THE AIR c1935 AFGP358

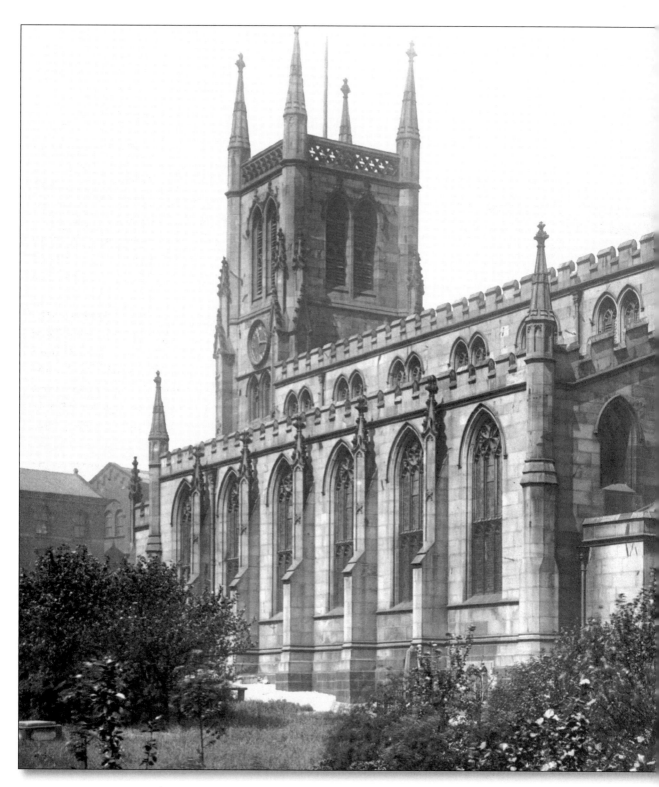

MIND, BODY AND SOUL

THE PARISH CHURCH 1894 34311

The care of people's souls was a concern of the authorities long before any provision was made for their educational, recreational or physical welfare. In this Blackburn was no exception. It is believed that the site of the parish church of St Mary has been associated with Christianity as far back as the 6th century. Evidence of a Norman church was discovered when the foundations for the new St Mary's were being dug in 1820.

By the 14th century St Mary's was an important church. It was rebuilt during Henry VIII's reign, but by 1818 it was in disrepair and inadequate for a town whose population was beginning to grow. The Manchester architect John Palmer was engaged to design the church, and the result was an imposing building in the Gothic revival style. The new St Mary's was consecrated in 1826.

View 34314 (page 49) looks towards the doors and western tower, where the peal of bells were hung. The church had been reseated and renovated in 1875. View 34313 (page 48-49) looks towards the altar and the great east window, which is said to have been brought from a Belgian convent. The figures in the bottom row are St Matthew, St Mark, the Blessed Virgin Mary, St Luke and St John, and in the upper row are St Andrew, St Philip, Jesus, St Matthias and St Simon Zelotes.

Manchester diocese had such a huge population by the 1920s that the case for dividing the diocese was compelling. Blackburn was chosen, in part for its central location; the diocese of Blackburn was created in 1926, and the former parish church of St Mary the Virgin became the cathedral. Blackburn was also chosen because there was room to extend the building in a manner befitting a cathedral. A fund was launched, and by 1933 there was enough money to commission an architect. W A Forsythe's plan was for the old parish church to form the nave of the enlarged cathedral in a modern version of the Gothic style. Work began in 1938; it was interrupted by the war, and continued in 1950 (B111002, pages 54-55). Forsythe died in 1961 and Laurence King took over, adapting some of his predecessor's plans. He designed the lantern tower with the sanctuary, or worshipping area, directly beneath it. Major work continued until the 1960s, but landscaping and other improvements continue to this day.

Above:
The Parish Church,
The Interior looking West 1894 34314

Left:
The Parish Church,
The Interior looking East 1894 34313

Mind, Body and Soul

The Parish Church 1923 74072

Two fine statues outside the parish church are pictured in the next two photographs - the church was three years yet from cathedral status at the date (1923) that 74072 (this page) and 74074 (page 52-53) were taken. In 74072 (above) we see the statue of Queen Victoria. Itself eleven feet high, it stands on a base which is fourteen feet high, and statue and base together weigh nearly forty tons. The statue was sculpted by Sir Bertram Mackennal; it was unveiled on 30 September 1905 by Princess Louise, Queen Victoria's fourth daughter. The statue of Gladstone (74074, pages 52-53) was unveiled on

4 November 1899 by the Earl of Aberdeen. It was sculpted by J Adams Acton, and was the first memorial statue in the country erected to Gladstone. It was found to be an obstruction to bus queues, and in 1955 it was removed to its present site outside the old technical college.

St John's Church (74078, pages 56-57) built in 1788 by subscription, was originally intended as a chapel of ease for St Mary's. The Sudell family crop up here again: Henry Sudell contributed half the cost. The tower is St John's dominant architectural feature, but it was not added until 1802, fourteen years after the church was built. The churchyard holds the remains of many of the town's principal merchants and manufacturers. The church closed in 1975, and is used now by community groups.

Popularly known as Pleasington Priory (34324, page 57) the Church of St Mary and St John the Baptist was opened on 24 August 1819. John Francis Butler of Pleasington Hall built the Priory. The tradition is that he had a riding accident on the site, and so he had the church built as a thanksgiving for his recovery. The architect was John Palmer; calling on a number of styles from Early English to Regency Gothic, he achieved an effect of venerable sanctity.

The development of the housing estate at Brownhill made urgent a need that had long been recognised. As early as 1889 a mission service had been held there in the back kitchen of a house in Whalley New Road. Later, a corrugated iron building was in use. The new church (B111027, page 57) was consecrated by Dr P M Herbert, Bishop of Blackburn, on 8 April 1933. Its modern design was much acclaimed, although by 1971 problems with damp and rotting timbers led to a major reconstruction.

The Church had been an early provider of education for ordinary folk, and there was resistance to the idea of education being provided by the state. The idea that further education should be provided encountered the stiffest opposition. When mechanics' institutes were first set up, there were those who thought the working classes were being educated beyond their station. Later, these same institutes were promoted as alternatives to the beer houses and inns. Even so, when a meeting was held in Blackburn in 1886 to discuss the building of a technical school, there was so little support that the idea was abandoned.

Science and art classes were available on a private basis in the town: these were provided by Dr T Isherwood, who held classes in St Peter Street and later in Paradise Lane, where he had a private school. His students went on to achieve success at Oxford University and Owens College, later Manchester University.

MIND, BODY AND SOUL

THE PARISH CHURCH AND THE GLADSTONE STATUE 1923 74074

Mind, Body and Soul

It was in 1887, the year of Queen Victoria's Golden Jubilee, that the idea of building a technical school was again put forward. The foundation stone was laid a year later on 9 May 1888 by the Prince and Princess of Wales. The chosen site was at Blakey Moor, an area of unsavoury slums.

The building opened for students in September 1891 (34309, pages 58-59). Most classes took place in the evenings. As might be expected, textiles figured largely, but there were also classes in engineering, building, physics, chemistry and art. Blackburn Education Committee assumed responsibility for the college in 1903. The 1918 Education Act led to an expansion of subjects into more commercial and academic areas.

The college expanded steadily. Room had to be found for classes in neighbouring buildings. Additional accommodation was built in Feilden Street in the 1950s and 60s, and the former Blakey Moor School was taken over for business and secretarial studies. The Nab Lane engineering building was opened in 1971, the School of Art in 1984 and the New Technology Centre in 1988. The college continues to expand; it now has over 24,000 part-time and 3,000 full-time students, compared to barely 700 in 1891.

Municipal provision of cultural and recreational facilities had to wait a little longer, but the wait was worthwhile. The public halls stand on a site which was occupied at the end of the 19th century by a notorious slum called Engine Street. The site was cleared so that King George V could lay the foundation stone for the halls on 10 July 1913. Work was interrupted by the First World War, but it continued soon afterwards at the request of the Local Government Board so as to provide employment. Most of the stone for the building came from the Butler Delph quarries at Pleasington, though the fluted shafts of the columns are Darley Dale stone and the steps to the entrances are of stone from the Shepley quarries near Huddersfield (74070, pages 60-61).

The halls were opened by Lord Derby on 21 October 1921 - on the same day he opened the new power station at Whitebirk. The accommodation comprised three halls: the Lecture Hall, the Assembly Hall, and King George's Hall. The Lecture Hall and the Assembly Hall had sprung floors for dancing, and a cinema screen was installed in King George's

THE CATHEDRAL c1950 B111002

The town's cathedral status is being made a reality as building work continues after the wartime interruption.

MIND, BODY AND SOUL

Hall. The halls were designed to function as separate units, but intercommunication was provided so that they could be used for one function. A memorial organ was installed - the ceremonial opening took place on 25 May 1922. Aldermen Nuttall and Cotton made large donations to the cost of the organ in memory of their sons, who had been killed in the First World War. The celebrated organist Marcel Dupre gave two recitals; the proceeds were put into the fund for assisting the village of Peronne, which was adopted by and later twinned with Blackburn.

A colonnade over the entrance to the police yard connected the public halls to the Sessions House, thus presenting an unbroken front of 380 feet. The Sessions House had opened in 1912. The first Quarter Sessions for the County Borough were held there on 26 July 1912; the police had moved into their new accommodation there a few days earlier.

Unless you could afford to pay, health care in Blackburn was fairly rudimentary in the early days of the town's development. A dispensary of sorts had existed in the town since at least the 18th century: a notice appearing in the Blackburn Mail for 1794 announces a meeting to consider appointing a doctor for the town's dispensary. It was at a later meeting in 1823 that a more ambitious scheme was launched. The Blackburn General Dispensary was opened on 1 February 1824, and in its first year it treated 1,813 people. This had increased to 4,658 by 1826, when among other ailments there were 89 cases of cholera, 40 cases of scarlet fever and 186 cases of smallpox.

Upon the introduction of the Poor Law Act in 1834 the dispensary closed, and care was transferred to the workhouse. Attempts had already been made to establish a fund to build an infirmary, but it had to wait until 1857, when William Pilkington was mayor, before a successful fund was launched. Pilkington laid the foundation stone for the Blackburn General Infirmary on Whit Monday, 24 May 1858. The event was celebrated by a balloon ascent. By 1861 the exterior of the building was complete, but the cotton famine caused by the American Civil War interrupted the work; it was not until the end of 1864 that the building was complete and fully equipped. In 1865, 246 in-patients and 270 out-patients were treated.

Nursing staff were originally resident in the Infirmary itself, but it was decided to provide separate accommodation. A nurses' home

was built in the grounds (43480, page 60) which was designed by Simpson and Duckworth of Blackburn and opened on 28 October 1893 by Mrs Harriet Harrison, founder and secretary of the Ladies' Infirmary Guild. She, together with her husband Henry, also a well-known philanthropist, paid for the cost of furnishing the building.

Almshouses as a means of accommodating the deserving poor have been a feature of English town life since Elizabethan times, particularly in towns with well-established parochial charities. In Blackburn, William and Jane Turner erected almshouses at Bank Top on the road to Witton Stocks in 1834, and in 1895 Nancy Derbyshire endowed six houses in St Silas's Road behind the church (35731, page 61).

Left:
ST JOHN'S CHURCH
1923 74078

Below Left:
PLEASINGTON PRIORY CHURCH
1894 34324

Below Right:
ST GABRIEL'S CHURCH, BROWNHILL c1955
B111027

The foundation stone for St Gabriel's was laid on 5 March 1932 by the Bishop of Blackburn, and just over a year later he was back for the consecration. The church had accommodation for 500 people. Its internal design echoed Norman architecture, with rectangular piers rising to a height of 25 feet and supporting a barrel-vaulted roof 40 feet from the floor.

MIND, BODY AND SOUL

THE TECHNICAL SCHOOL 1894 34309

The building had three floors and a basement, which housed the textile department. Commercial engineering, physics, and cookery were on the ground floor, chemistry on the first floor, and the art department on the second floor. There were sheds at the back for spinning, weaving, winding, warping and sizing.

MIND, BODY AND SOUL

Left:
THE PUBLIC HALLS AND THE SESSIONS HOUSE
1923 74070

The architects Briggs and Wolstenholme and Stones & Stones, both with offices in Blackburn and Liverpool, drew up designs for the public halls. The halls were heated by hot water, and had ventilating machinery which added ozone to the fresh air distributed throughout the building. There were electric lights, and emergency gas lights.

Below Left:
THE NURSES' HOME 1899 43480

The home provided accommodation for 30 nurses and 2 domestics. There were sitting rooms, a reading room and a recreation room. The former nurses' quarters in the infirmary were converted into patient accommodation, providing 13 extra beds.

Below Right:
THE ALMSHOUSES 1895 35731

The houses, endowed by Nancy Derbyshire, were designed by Stones and Gradwell of Blackburn. They were built of stone, and had a porch, a living room, 2 bedrooms, a scullery and an outside toilet. There were gardens to front and rear. Those chosen to occupy the houses were granted a weekly allowance of 7 shillings (35p). The almshouses were formally opened on 20 June 1895 by James Hargreaves, chairman of the trustees.

ORDNANCE SURVEY MAP SHOWING BLACKBURN AND SURROUNDING AREAS 1892

THE PARKS

Above:
CORPORATION PARK, THE LAKE
1923 74067

Left:
CORPORATION PARK, THE LAKE
1895 35727

Creating a green space in the town became ever more desirable as the ill effects of industrialisation became apparent. Blackburn as much as anywhere needed somewhere where people could go to escape the rows and rows of terraced housing and the proliferating forest of smoking chimneys.

The lake (74067, above and 35727, left) was created in 1840 before the park opened. Later it was stocked with ducks and geese donated by local people. Alderman Cunningham donated two black swans, which adapted well to the environment and survived for several generations. Subsequent attempts to introduce other swans

were not so successful. Note the children on the left of 74067 (left) feeding the ducks. The lake was overlooked by the grand houses of East Park Road (35727, below left).

The land occupied by Corporation Park was bought from Joseph Feilden, lord of the manor, in 1855 at a cost of £50 per acre; fifty acres altogether were acquired. The town's water supply had been there – there were two small reservoirs fed by Pemberton Clough. Later, in 1847, Blackburn Waterworks Company supplied the town from reservoirs at Guide, Audley, Pickup Bank and Daisyfield.

Blackburn received its charter of incorporation in 1851, and the town's early mayors were keen to adopt public works. Thomas Dugdale, who was mayor from 1854 to 1855, proposed establishing a public park. The Council agreed to bear the cost of constructing roads on either side of the park, but they were able to recoup some of the cost by selling land on the town's moor at Nova Scotia to the East Lancashire and Blackburn Railway Company. Work on the roads commenced in February 1855.

William Henderson, a landscape gardener from Birkenhead, was engaged to supervise the laying out of the grounds, which he did with the assistance of Mr P McGregor and Mr T Jenkins. The Blackburn contractors Roberts & Walmsley built the entrance gateway and the lodge. The perimeter walls were built by Thomas and John Holden and William Wright, all of Blackburn, using stone from quarries in the park. The promenades, bowling greens and carriage roads were constructed by James Taylor of Burnley.

The Broad Walk (74061, pages 70-71) was constructed in the 1860s, 10 years before the photograph was taken. Broad Walk had been lined with children, there to cheer the progress of the visiting King George V. The Broad Walk had a moment of drama in the Second World War: a Spitfire crashed in Blackburn in 1944. The pilot bailed out and parachuted to safety, landing on the Broad Walk.

Thursday 22 October 1857 was the day chosen for the park's opening. It was a fine, crisp, frosty day. It is said that every man, woman and child in the borough turned out, as well as visitors from towns and villages from miles around. Certainly the railway companies laid on special excursions, and claimed that 14,000 people travelled to the town. Shops and mills closed, church bells were ringing and there were flags flying from every public building.

CORPORATION PARK 1895 35729

William Pilkington would have been pleased to see the park so well
used 40 years after his inaugural speech. There is not a spare bench
seat to be had. Something about the smart attire of the people
and the full leaf of the trees suggests a summer Sunday afternoon,
though the gentleman with his umbrella is taking no chances.

CORPORATION PARK 1923 74060

A less crowded scene. How many Blackburn babies must have
taken their first breaths of fresh air in Corporation park? There are
plenty of babies in 74061, too, on pages 70-71.

CORPORATION PARK, THE BROAD WALK 1923 74061

Far Left:
CORPORATION PARK
THE TENNIS COURTS 1923 74065

Left:
THE VIEW FROM THE TENNIS
COURTS c1950 B111009

The tennis courts were created in 1920.
Note how propriety demanded that
ladies wore hats even when playing tennis
(74065). View B111009 shows a fine
view of the town, giving some idea of how
steeply the park climbs up the hill.

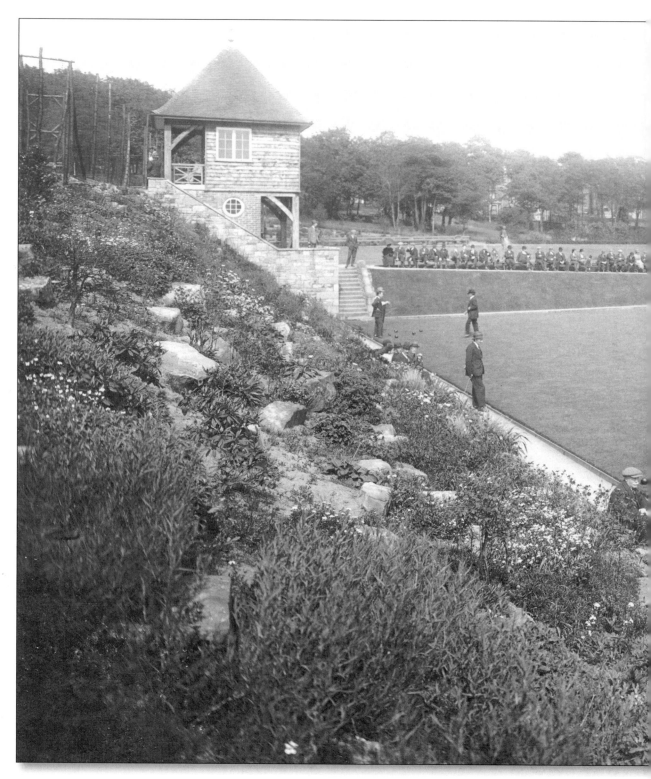

CORPORATION PARK, THE BOWLING GREEN 1923 74064

The first two of the park's three bowling greens were laid out in 1923, and the third in 1925, so this green cannot have been many weeks old when this match was being played. Note the attentive and no doubt highly critical spectators in the background.

Above:
CORPORATION PARK
1923 74055

Right:
THE GARDEN OF REMEMBRANCE
c1955 B111008

Plans for a Garden of Remembrance were made in 1922. Photograph 74055 showing the chosen site was taken a year before the war memorial was unveiled there by Mrs M J Brown, who had lost four sons in the Great War. The peaceful scene is a tribute to the gardener's art. The spire of Trinity Methodist Church can be seen above the trees in B111008.

Above:
CORPORATION PARK
THE CONSERVATORY 1923 74069

The conservatory was opened on 16 May 1900.
A banana plant had produced fruit there by
1903. Plans for heating the conservatory had only
recently been approved in 1921.

Left:
CORPORATION PARK
THE CONSERVATORY 1923 74062

THE PARKS

CORPORATION PARK
THE BANDSTAND 1923 74058

Crowds gathered in front of the town hall to watch the procession. George Ellis's band led the way, followed by a detachment of police, then the halberd bearers, then Mayor William Pilkington with Aldermen Dugdale and Hoole. The other aldermen followed with councillors and invited guests. Clergymen followed them, and then came the magistrates, the pupils from the Grammar School led by the headmaster, the Rechabites with the Darwen Temperance Band, and the United Catholic Brethren with Mr Finney's United Brass Band. Another detachment of police brought up the rear.

The entrance to the park had been decorated with dahlias and evergreens. The driveways were lined with spectators. When the procession arrived, the cannon in the battery at the top of the park manned by men of the Royal Artillery were fired. The procession was half a mile long. It wound its way through the park until it reached the platform erected above the lake; it was from this point that the park was to be declared open.

Shortly after three o'clock in the afternoon, William Pilkington mounted the platform and addressed the crowd, which was estimated at 8,000 strong. He hailed the park as both a moral and physical boon to the inhabitants of Blackburn, especially the poorer classes. He expressed his certainty that 'generations yet unborn will have cause to bless the day when this noble and beautiful park was established'. At this point a balloon was launched, and the crowd cheered. He concluded with his opinion that Blackburn was now on an equal footing with any neighbouring town.

After prolonged cheers and further reports from the cannon, former Mayor Alderman Dugdale rose to speak. He congratulated the mayor for his efforts and generosity in promoting causes for the public good, and expressed the hope that old and young, rich and poor would use the park for rational and innocent amusement.

There were speeches from Alderman Cunningham and Alderman Baynes. Sir W Henry Feilden concluded the ceremony, and the procession reassembled and withdrew in the same order in which it had entered the park. The cannon continued to roar, accompanied by the firing of private firearms to 'the great waste of powder, and to the alarm and headache of many old, infirm, quiet, and nervous people', as an observer remarked. A dinner was served in the Town Hall Assembly room for 200 guests, and in the evening crowds reassembled in the park for a firework display conducted by Mr Bywater of Sheffield; one of the principal attractions was an illuminated device bearing the words 'The People's Park'.

View 74058 (page 76-77) shows Corporation Park's second band stand (the first, built in 1880, was demolished at the turn of the century). This one was opened on 17 September 1909 by Councillor J Higginson, vice-chairman of the Parks Committee. Seating was provided for over 2,000, but as we can see in the background, many more than that could stand or sit on the grass to listen to the programme of Sunday concerts.

Flora was the Roman goddess of flowers and spring, and her statue (35730, right) was sculpted by Thomas Allen of Liverpool and presented by T H Fairhurst in 1871. There is a legend that on certain nights of the year Flora descends from her pedestal and roams the park. Maybe this is a story that owes its origins to the effects of strong liquor on lonely revellers wandering homewards after an enjoyable evening.

There were originally four fountains in the park. Mayor William Pilkington paid for three, which were built in 1857. The one near the main entrance (34319, pages 60-61) was the largest. The fourth one, which was sited in the stream that ran through the park, was paid for by John Dean. The jet from the fountain we see in 34319 soared twenty feet, and its spray was an inconvenience to those seated nearby. The fountains ceased to function early in the 1900s.

The site for Queen's Park (B111020, pages 80-81) was acquired by the Corporation from the Ecclesiastical Commissioners in 1882 on condition that it be used only as a public park and ornamental garden. It was laid out at a cost of £10,000, and was opened to the public in June 1887. The park originally boasted two bowling greens and two tennis courts, along with a lake over 3 acres in extent (43485, pages 82-83 and B111018, pages 84-85) a children's paddling pool, a band stand and a refreshment room. In 1932 two additional bowling greens and a pavilion

CORPORATION PARK,
THE STATUE OF FLORA 1895 35730

CORPORATION PARK 1923 74052

This is the Preston New Road entrance, a grand archway, symbolic of Blackburn's aspirations as a booming cotton town. The trees were planted in 1869. The significance of the park to young and old alike is evident in this picture.

were provided, and in 1936 the Corporation took over the boating rights to the lake, which had previously been let, bought modern boats and refurbished the refreshment rooms.

The lake was opened in November 1888. It occupied the roughest terrain in the park, which would have been hard to put to any other use. It followed a serpentine course, and there was a wooden footbridge, crowded with spectators in 43485, pages 82-83. A landing space for 20 boats was provided. Boats were still on the lake in the 1950s, though none are in evidence on B111018, pages 84-85. In the background are the buildings and chimney of Queen's Park Hospital, most of which are now demolished.

Roe Lee Park (B111024, page 85) was opened on Wednesday 30 May 1923. It occupied 16 acres of land which were given to the town by Messrs Duckworth & Eddleston of Roe Lee Mills, and the park was intended to commemorate the visit of King George V to Blackburn in 1913. Duckworth & Eddleston granted their employees a half-day holiday, and flags flew from their mills. John Duckworth officiated, opening the pavilion with a gold key handed to him by the Borough Engineer, which he later presented to the Mayor. The park had 5 tennis courts and 3 bowling greens.

Blackburn was later to provide even more open spaces for its citizens in 1946 when it bought Witton Park, the ancestral home of the Feilden family. The local benefactor R E Hart contributed generously to this project. Covering 400 acres, Witton Park was larger than all the town's other parks and playing fields put together.

The Parks

CORPORATION PARK
THE FOUNTAIN 1894 34319

The Parks

THE PARKS

Right: QUEEN'S PARK, THE LAKE c1955 B111018

Below Left: QUEEN'S PARK c1955 B111020

The site for the park had once been unenclosed moorland, exposed to every wind that blew. This photograph shows how careful tree planting and the skill of the gardeners transformed it.

Below Right: ROE LEE PARK c1955 B111024

The pavilion was built by Fecitt & Sons. It was well-equipped for tennis and bowls players, and it had refreshment rooms in the middle. The four-dialled clock in the tower was visible from all over the park.

INDEX

Names of Subscribers

The following people have kindly supported this book by purchasing limited edition copies prior to publication.

In memory of Mrs E A Ashworth, Blackburn

Bill Aspin

Dave and Sue Baldwin - Together again

Mr F Barton, Blackburn, Happy birthday Dad

Mr C G E and Mrs C Beardmore, Blackburn

To Josephine Cox, our thanks, Jean and Bernard

As a tribute to the Bibby family, from Joyce

Mr and Mrs Birchall

The Blades family, Oswaldtwistle

In memory of Tony Blundell, Bridgend

Mrs Hilda Boardman, Blackburn

Alexander and Doreen Bunting and Family

In Memory of Ted and Joyce Cannon

Brian Carbery, Blackburn, on Father's Day

Harold and Connie Carter, Blackburn

In memory of Alice Clarke, née Jarrett

Eileen and Ray Connoley, Llanvaches, Wales

Dacia Cook, Blackburn

Peter Cooper, Blackburn

Rachel and Matthew Cottam of Blackburn

Malcom Croasdale

Cyril Crossley, Blackburn

David Crossley, Blackburn

The Crossley Family, Rishton

The Crossley Family, Rishton, Lancashire

Councillor Alan Dean

George Duckworth

In memory of Mary and Edward Dudgeon

Mr K and Mrs L Dunn

Mr M and Mrs H Eccles, Blackburn

May Etherington

As a tribute to our parents, Ralph and Evelyn

Hilary and Mick Farrer, Carlisle

John and Brenda Ferguson

In memory of the Firbank Family, Blackburn

John Fleming, Whalley

Nicholas Ford, for his 76th Birthday

Michel and Martine Garnier, Vichy

Tom Gavin

The Geraghty Family, Blackburn

Vincent and Eileen Gillett, Blackburn

The Goodall Family, Rishton

The Grimshaw Family, Blackburn

In memory of Alderman George Haworth

Geoff Leaver-Heaton - from brother, Trevor

James Hinnigan

Mr and Mrs J Hindle and Family, Blackburn

Michael and Carolyn Hogan, Blackburn

Walter I Hubert

The Hunt Family, Rishton, Blackburn

John Hyde, Blackburn

The Ismail Family, Blackburn

Keepsake of Norman and Margaret Jackson's Family

Mrs Susan Jackson

Heather Jenkinson, Blackburn

Ian Jenkinson, Bare, formerly Blackburn

Frank M Kay, Blackburn

Mr D M and Mrs J E Kippax, Blackburn

Bruce and Marian Kitchin, Blackburn

Renee Knowles

Mr W Lamb and Mrs Freda Lamb, Blackburn

David Lawson

The Leaver-Heaton Family, Blackburn

Anthony Lockley

Adrienne Longworth, née Hull

The Lucas Family, Blackburn

In Memory of Frank and Irene Maudsley
John and Chris McCherry, Australia
Sonia McLoughlin née Lord, Blackburn
Lynne and Kevin Mills, Blackburn
To Brenda in NZ, Happy Christmas, love Miriam
To my brother Tony, Happy Christmas, Miriam
Anthony Moorcroft
Mildred Moorcroft
Valerie Joan Murtagh
Margery Nowell
In memory of John Oddie of Blackburn
Roy O'Malley
John Peters, Rishton, born in Blackburn
John Peters, To dad on your 75th birthday
Mr D C and Mrs D Phillips, Blackburn
Trevor Porter
Mr E N and Mrs V R Price of Blackburn
The Samuels Family, Blackburn
Mr and Mrs W Shepherd
Raymond and Maureen Slater

Arthur Smith
Valerie Smith, Thornton
W H Smith
Smokers World
D C Stellenboom and A Stellenboom, Blackburn
Mr and Mrs R H Sunner, Blackburn
Leonard Sutter
The Svarc Family, Blackburn
Mrs Ann L Szandurski - Romer
Doreen M Turner, Blackburn
Mr D J Walter
James Ward
Mr D and Mrs M Ward, Blackburn
The Weall Family, Blackburn
Arthur Witherington
The Woodruff Family, Blackburn

FRITH PRODUCTS & SERVICES

Francis Frith would doubtless be pleased to know that the pioneering publishing venture he started in 1860 still continues today. Over a hundred and forty years later, The Francis Frith Collection continues in the same innovative tradition and is now one of the foremost publishers of vintage photographs in the world. Some of the current activities include:

Interior Decoration

Today Frith's photographs can be seen framed and as giant wall murals in thousands of pubs, restaurants, hotels, banks, retail stores and other public buildings throughout the country. In every case they enhance the unique local atmosphere of the places they depict and provide reminders of gentler days in an increasingly busy and frenetic world.

Product Promotions

Frith products are used by many major companies to promote the sales of their own products or to reinforce their own history and heritage. Frith promotions have been used by Hovis bread, Courage beers, Scots Porage Oats, Colman's mustard, Cadbury's foods, Mellow Birds coffee, Dunhill pipe tobacco, Guinness, and Bulmer's Cider.

Genealogy and Family History

As the interest in family history and roots grows world-wide, more and more people are turning to Frith's photographs of Great Britain for images of the towns, villages and streets where their ancestors lived; and, of course, photographs of the churches and chapels where their ancestors were christened, married and buried are an essential part of every genealogy tree and family album.

Frith Products

All Frith photographs are available Framed or just as Mounted Prints and Posters (size 23 x 16 inches). These may be ordered from the address below. From time to time other products - Address Books, Calendars, Table Mats, etc - are available.

The Internet

Already ninety thousand Frith photographs can be viewed and purchased on the internet through the Frith websites and a myriad of partner sites.

For more detailed information on Frith companies and products, look at these sites:

www.francisfrith.co.uk
www.francisfrith.com
(for North American visitors)

See the complete list of Frith Books at:

www.francisfrith.co.uk

This web site is regularly updated with the latest list of publications from The Francis Frith Collection. If you wish to buy books relating to another part of the country that your local bookshop does not stock, you may purchase on-line.

For further information, trade, or author enquiries please contact us at the address below:
The Francis Frith Collection, Frith's Barn, Teffont, Salisbury, Wiltshire, England SP3 5QP.
Tel: +44 (0)1722 716 376 Fax: +44 (0)1722 716 881   Email: sales@francisfrith.co.uk

---

See Frith books on the internet at www.francisfrith.co.uk

FREE PRINT OF YOUR CHOICE

Mounted Print
Overall size 14 x 11 inches (355 x 280mm)

Choose any Frith photograph in this book.
Simply complete the Voucher opposite and return it with your remittance for £2.25 (to cover postage and handling) and we will print the photograph of your choice in SEPIA (size 11 x 8 inches) and supply it in a cream mount with a burgundy rule line (overall size 14 x 11 inches).
Please note: photographs with a reference number starting with a "Z" are not Frith photographs and cannot be supplied under this offer.
Offer valid for delivery to one UK address only.

PLUS: **Order additional Mounted Prints at HALF PRICE - £7.49 each** (normally £14.99)
If you would like to order more Frith prints from this book, possibly as gifts for friends and family, you can buy them at half price (with no additional postage and handling costs).

PLUS: **Have your Mounted Prints framed**
For an extra £14.95 per print you can have your mounted print(s) framed in an elegant polished wood and gilt moulding, overall size 16 x 13 inches (no additional postage and handling required).

IMPORTANT!

These special prices are only available if you use this form to order . You must use the ORIGINAL VOUCHER on this page (no copies permitted). We can only despatch to one UK address. This offer cannot be combined with any other offer.

Send completed Voucher form to:
The Francis Frith Collection, Frith's Barn, Teffont, Salisbury, Wiltshire SP3 5QP

CHOOSE A PHOTOGRAPH FROM THIS BOOK

Voucher for *FREE* and Reduced Price Frith Prints

Please do not photocopy this voucher. Only the original is valid, so please fill it in, cut it out and return it to us with your order.

Picture ref no	Page no	Qty	Mounted @ £7.49	Framed + £14.95	Total Cost £
		1	Free of charge*	£	£
			£7.49	£	£
			£7.49	£	£
			£7.49	£	£
			£7.49	£	£
			£7.49	£	£

Please allow 28 days for delivery. Offer available to one UK address only

* Post & handling	£3.50
Total Order Cost	£

Title of this book . . . .
I enclose a cheque/postal order for £ . . . .
made payable to 'The Francis Frith Collection'

OR please debit my Mastercard / Visa / Maestro / Amex card, details below

Card Number

Issue No (Maestro only)   Valid from (Maestro)

Expires   Signature

Name Mr/Mrs/Ms . . . .
Address . . . .
. . . .
. . . .
. . . . Postcode . . . .
Daytime Tel No . . . .
Email . . . .

ISBN 1-85937-986-9   Valid to 31/12/08

Can you help us with information about any of the Frith photographs in this book?

We are gradually compiling an historical record for each of the photographs in the Frith archive. It is always fascinating to find out the names of the people shown in the pictures, as well as insights into the shops, buildings and other features depicted.

If you recognize anyone in the photographs in this book, or if you have information not already included in the author's caption, do let us know. We would love to hear from you, and will try to publish it in future books or articles.

Our production team

Frith books are produced by a small dedicated team at offices in the converted Grade II listed 18th-century barn at Teffont near Salisbury, illustrated above. Most have worked with the Frith Collection for many years. All have in common one quality: they have a passion for the Frith Collection. The team is constantly expanding, but currently includes:

Paul Baron, Jason Buck, John Buck, Heather Crisp, David Davies, Louis du Mont, Isobel Hall, Lucy Hart, Julian Hight, Peter Horne, James Kinnear, Karen Kinnear, Tina Leary, Stuart Login, Sue Molloy, Sarah Roberts, Kate Rotondetto, Dean Scource, Eliza Sackett, Terence Sackett, Sandra Sampson, Adrian Sanders, Sandra Sanger, Julia Skinner, Miles Smith, Lewis Taylor, Shelley Tolcher, Lorraine Tuck, Miranda Tunnicliffe, David Turner and Ricky Williams.